2021
MONTREAL
Restaurants

The Food Enthusiast's Long Weekend Guide

Andrew Delaplaine

GET 3 FREE NOVELS
Like political thrillers?
See next page to download 3 FREE page-turning novels—no strings attached.

*Andrew Delaplaine is the Food Enthusiast.
When he's not playing tennis,
he dines anonymously
at the Publisher's (considerable) expense.*

WANT 3 FREE THRILLERS?

Why, of course you do!
If you like these writers--
Vince Flynn, Brad Thor, Tom Clancy, James Patterson, David Baldacci, John Grisham, Brad Meltzer, Daniel Silva, Don DeLillo
If you like these TV series –
House of Cards, Scandal, West Wing, The Good Wife, Madam Secretary, Designated Survivor

> You'll love the **unputdownable** series about Jack Houston St. Clair, with political intrigue, romance, and loads of action and suspense.

Besides writing travel books, I've written political thrillers for many years that have delighted hundreds of thousands of readers. I want to introduce you to my work!
Send me an email and I'll send you a link where you can download the first 3 books in my bestselling series, absolutely FREE.
Mention **this book** when you email me.

andrewdelaplaine@mac.com
Gramercy Park Press
New York - London – Paris
Cover Photo by Matthieu Joannon on Unsplash
Copyright © by Gramercy Park Press - All rights reserved.

MONTREAL

The Food Enthusiast's Complete Restaurant Guide

Table of Contents

Introduction – 5

The A to Z Listings – 11
Ridiculously Extravagant
Sensible Alternatives
Quality Bargain Spots

Food Markets – 77

Index – 83
(includes Cuisine Index)

Other Books by the Food Enthusiast - 89

Introduction

DID YOU FIND AN INTERESTING PLACE?
If you discover a place you think I should check out on my next visit, drop me a line, will you? I'll mention your name if I end up listing it.
andrewdelaplaine@mac.com

Though Quebec has all those quaint little streets and more properly looks like it belongs in a theme park than in the real world, Montreal is really where all the action is in this mostly French-speaking Canadian province.

This location has always been an economic center, first settled by the Iroquois, and then by the French when they arrived in 1535.

Two hundred years later, the English took control when they defeated the French, giving Montreal a fascinating cultural history that is reflected in the enormous diversity we find there today.

Despite the British victory in the field, the "French" part of Canada couldn't be stronger. This city has more native-born French speakers than any city in the world besides Paris.

Certain specialties you'll want to seek out: *poutine* (which is basically French fries with a generous dollop of gravy-sauce with cheese curds added), deep-fried foie gras, Portuguese chicken, bagels made in the distinctive Montreal style and smoked meats.

POUTINE

This dish is served as a fast food in Canada (even in the hockey arenas and at certain McDonald's), and can be almost as revolting as its description sounds, but when done with care and creativity, it's a masterpiece of simple culinary joy. When it's done right, the fries will be crispy (not leaden, thick and mealy), and the sauce-gravy will be rich and flavorful.

Good places to get it are:
Patati Patata
4177 Blvd St-Laurent, 514-844-0216
No web site
and
La Banquise
994 Rue Rachel East, 514-525-2415
http://labanquise.com/

The portions are larger here, and they're open 24 hours.

BAGELS

Not to be confused with the New York version you're probably more familiar with. These are boiled in water laced with honey and made with eggs and unsalted dough. They are cooked in a wood-burning oven. The holes are larger and the overall size is smaller. The surface is not as shiny as New York bagels. I like them sprinkled with sesame seeds.

Good places to get them are:

Fairmont Bagel
74 Ave. Fairmount West, 514-272-0667
www.fairmountbagel.com
and
St-Viateur Bagel
263 Ave. St-Viateur West, 514-276-8044
www.stviateurbagel.com

SMOKED MEATS

Jews from Eastern Europe are responsible for bringing this concept to Montreal decades ago. It is beef brisket marinated for days in a rich brine and spices that's been steamed and hot-smoked and it's very, very tasty, especially if you specify that you want the meat fatty. Your first bite causes the taste buds in your mouth to explode. Best served with any excellent mustard, pickles and cold beer. (Do not call this corned beef – it's smoked meat.)

Good places to get it are:
The Main Deli Steakhouse
3864 Blvd St-Laurent, 514-843-8126
www.maindelisteakhouse.com
and
Schwartz's Montreal Hebrew Delicatessen
3895 Blvd St-Laurent, 514-842-4813 / cash only
www.schwartzsdeli.com

PORTUGUESE CHICKEN

In Portugal, this dish is called "African chicken," not Portuguese chicken. It's just a simple whole chicken cooked in a rotisserie or grilled and there's usually a chili rub or some other spices added. It's served up by the substantial sub-culture of Portuguese-Canadians here in Montreal.

Good places to get it are:
Rotisserie Romados
115 rue Rachel East, 514- 849-1803
http://romados.ca/ - **web-site down at press time**

Don't let the stark fluorescent lights put you off. Or the long lines. The service is swift and the line moves rapidly. If you think you're leaving, take one deep breath and the aromas will keep you where you belong.

And also--
Portugalia
34 rue Rachel West, 514- 282-1519
www.rotisserieportugalia.com

Simple service at the blue-tiled counter. Here the chicken is butterflied and daubed with a hot chili paste and other condiments. Scrumptious.

FRIED FOIE GRAS

They take the goose or duck liver, bread it and then pop it into a deep fryer. Sounds terribly bad for your heart, right? Well, it is.

Two of the best examples of this are at **Joe Beef** and **Au Pied de Cochon** – see listings below.

Montreal has had its ups and downs as the province flirted with independence (there was a vote as recently as 1995 that was narrowly defeated), causing a lot of companies to bail out and move their headquarters to Toronto.

But Montreal has nevertheless always been a wonderful place to visit. Its rich history and cultural melting pot have combined to give the restaurant scene here everything the confirmed food fanatic might desire.

The A to Z Listings
Ridiculously Extravagant
Sensible Alternatives
Quality Bargain Spots

DID YOU FIND AN INTERESTING PLACE?
If you discover a place you think I should check out on my next visit, drop me a line, will you? I'll mention your name if I end up listing it.
andrewdelaplaine@mac.com

ACCORDS
22, rue Sainte-Catherine Est, Montréal , 514-508-2122
www.accords.ca
CUISINE: French / Wine Bar
DRINKS: Full Bar

SERVING: Lunch & Dinner daily, Closed Sun
PRICE RANGE: $$$
This is primarily a wine bar with a seasonal eclectic menu for wine and food pairing. The breads and desserts are house-made and the coffee is organic. The brick-walled outdoor patio in good weather is great, a snug little hideaway in the big bad town of Montreal. Menu favorites include: Agnolotti stuffed with guinea fowl confit and Cornish hen.

AGRIKOL
1844 Rue Amherst, Montreal, 514-903-6707
www.agrikol.ca
CUISINE: Haitian
DRINKS: Full Bar
SERVING: Dinner
PRICE RANGE: $$
NEIGBORHHOOD: Villa-Marie
Authentic Creole and Haitian cuisine. Different menus for inside and outside on the patio (BBQ). You can watch the bartender press sugar cane to extract the juice used to make some of the creative rum drinks. The name Agrikol is derived from a rum made with cane juice, by the way. The décor here is very lovely, with peach-colored walls and palm fronds painted on them to give you a sense of the tropics from which the cuisine is inspired. (It'll make you were wish you points south, too, in the endless winter months.) My Menupicks: Beef cheek and Short rib stew. Unique cocktails like the Dark 'n Stormy made with ginger beer and dark rum.

AMIR
580 Rue Sainte-Catherine E, Montreal, 514-849-2647
www.restoamir.com
CUISINE: Lebanese
DRINKS: No Booze
SERVING: Open Daily
PRICE RANGE: $$
This Lebanese-style Middle Eastern fast food chain with counter service serves delicious food like shish taouk. Here you'll find shawarma sandwiches, falafel, hummus, and tabbouleh. Several locations in the Montreal area.

ARTHUR'S NOSH BAR
4621 Rue Notre Dame O, Montreal, 514-757-5190
www.arthursmtl.com
CUISINE: Canadian (New)
DRINKS: Full Bar
SERVING: Dinner; closed Sun, Mon & Tues
PRICE RANGE: $$$$
NEIGBORHHOOD: Sud-Ouest
Jewish classics served with a twist. My Favorites: Latke Smorgasbord and Avo Toast. Or try the Moroccan toast with Israeli salad, chickpeas and an egg topping it off. Communal tables and bar seating.

AU PIED DE COCHON
536 Avenue Duluth Est, Montréal, 514-281-1114
www.restaurantaupieddecochon.ca
CUISINE: Argentinean
DRINKS: Full Bar
SERVING: Breakfast, Brunch, Late night
PRICE RANGE: $$
Chef Martin Picard offers his menu of hearty Québécois fare. My Menu Favorites include: Foie gras & pork and the Happy Pork Chop. Extensive wine list.

BEAUTY'S
93 Avenue du Mont-Royal Ouest, Montreal, 514-849-8883
www.beautys.ca
CUISINE: Diner / Breakfast
DRINKS: Full Bar
SERVING: Open Daily, Breakfast, Brunch
PRICE RANGE: $$

This authentic vintage diner (they opened in the 1940s) offers a friendly atmosphere and a typical diner-style menu. My Menu Favorites include: Banana pancakes and Spicy Turkey Burger. The old guy greeting guests at the door is the owner, Hymie, now in his 90s. He bought this place in 1942 for $500. Son Larry helps run the place.

BIG IN JAPAN
4175 Boulevard Saint-Laurent, Montréal, 514-380-5658
No Website
CUISINE: Japanese
DRINKS: Full Bar
SERVING: Lunch Weekdays, Dinner nightly, late night
PRICE RANGE: $$

This casual diner-inspired eatery has an unusual look. Dozens of votive candles light the place (there's no electric light as far as I could tell), so it's dark and romantic. The smooth blond wood lining the walls is soft and relaxing. Curtains create little enclaves. The curving bar is another visual treat. People who are serious about their craft cocktails are at this bar. They offer a menu of Japanese treats, sandwiches and desserts. My Menu Favorites include: Curry Braised pork and Mibo Nasu & Miso ramen. Not authentic Japanese cuisine but the portions are large and tasty.

BORIS BISTRO
465 Rue McGill, Montréal, 514-848-9575
www.borisbistro.com
CUISINE: French
DRINKS: Full Bar
SERVING: Lunch, Dinner, Open daily
PRICE RANGE: $$$
Here diners enjoying an alfresco dining terrace behind a freestanding façade. The extensive French menu offers a variety of classics but also includes some creative dishes and a vegan plate. My Menu Favorites include the Red Tuna and Duck risotto with oyster mushrooms. Note this restaurant forbids children and minors inside the restaurant however they are allowed to dine on the terrace if accompanied by an adult. Hours are limited during winter.

BOUILLION BILK
1595 Boulevard Saint-Laurent, Montreal, 514-845-1595
www.bouillonbilk.com
CUISINE: Canadian cuisine
DRINKS: Full Bar
SERVING: Lunch & Dinner daily
PRICE RANGE: $$$

This popular fine-dining eatery is a must stop if you're attending an event at the nearby Quartier des Spectacles. It doesn't look very promising with the low-cost electronics stores nearby and the punk bar down the street, but don't let that dissuade you. There's serious cooking going on here. The décor gives off a sleek Scandinavian vibe. The impressive menu includes great dishes like Foie Gras, one of their most popular dishes. My Menu Favorites include: Lobster and Octopus & Sweetbread and my favorite, bone marrow with snails. Reservations a must.

BRASSERIE BERNARD
1249 Avenue Bernard, Montréal, 514-508-5519
www.brasseriebernard.com/?lang=en
CUISINE: French/Canadian (New)
DRINKS: Full Bar
SERVING: Lunch & Dinner
PRICE RANGE: $$$
Stylish Parisian-inspired bistro with a menu to match. The brunch on the weekends is especially good, with café au lait and eggs Benedict perennial favorites. Other popular picks include: Duck Confit and Beef Tartar. Impressive selection of wines. (The excellent service is worth noting as well.)

BRASSERIE T
1425 Rue Jeanne-Mance, Montreal, 514-282-0808
www.brasserie-t.com
CUISINE: French / Brasserie
DRINKS: Full Bar
SERVING: Lunch & Dinner daily
PRICE RANGE: $$$
This chic French eatery is an ideal choice for pre-theatre dining. The menu is small but tasty. My Menu Favorites include: Salmon Tartare and Shrimp Guedille. But I invariably end up ordering the steak frites because the herb butter they use is so delectably sublime. Patio is a great place for dining when weather permits.

BUVETTE CHEZ DIMONE
4869 Avenue du Parc, Montréal, 514-750-6577
www.buvettechezsimone.com
CUISINE: Wine Bar / Café
DRINKS: Full Bar
SERVING: Dinner
PRICE RANGE: $$
This cute wine bar offers an impressive rotating list of wines and a Tapas menu. My Menu Favorites include the Oysters with Bloody Caesar sauce and the creative charcuterie platters. This is a great opportunity to order several half portions to taste the many unique dishes.

BYBLOS LE PETIT CAFÉ
1499 Avenue Laurier Est, Montréal, 514-523-9396
www.byblospetitcafe.com
CUISINE: Middle Eastern
DRINKS: Full Bar
SERVING: Breakfast, Brunch, Dinner
PRICE RANGE: $$

This artsy Middle Eastern coffeehouse offers a menu featuring Persian dishes, fragrant stews, and dips served with pita. Here you'll find lots of sweet breads, feta cheese, and omelets. Try the Iranian tea for a treat with dessert.

CAFÉ LES ENTRETIENS
1577 Avenue Laurier Est, Montréal, 514-521-2934
www.cafelesentretiens.com
CUISINE: Café / Canadian cuisine
DRINKS: Full Bar
SERVING: Breakfast, Lunch, Dinner
PRICE RANGE: $$

This relaxed neighborhood eatery offers a romantic café atmosphere like one would expect to find in Paris. Here you'll find a nice simple menu with a nice selection of soups, salads, pastas, burgers and sandwiches. Occasional live music. Great dessert selection.

CAFÉ SANTROPOL
3990 Rue Saint-Urbain, Montreal, 514-842-3110
www.santropol.com
CUISINE: Vegetarian
DRINKS: No Booze
SERVING: Lunch, Dinner
PRICE RANGE: $$
This quaint café offers a friendly atmosphere including an outdoor patio (open in warmer months). The vegetarian menu offers a variety of healthy sandwiches.

CHIPOLE & JALAPENO
1481 Rue Amherst, Montréal, 514-523-6000
www.chipotleandjalapenomenu.ca/
CUISINE: Mexican
DRINKS: Full Bar
SERVING: Lunch, Dinner, Open daily
PRICE RANGE: $$
This place serves authentic Mexican cuisine like Puntas a la Mexicana. My Menu Favorites include the Fajitas and the Tortilla soup.

CREMERIE DALLA ROSE
4609 Rue Notre-Dame O, Montreal, 514-846-1555
www.dallarose.ca
CUISINE: Ice cream/Frozen Yogurt
DRINKS: No Booze
SERVING: 12 – 10 p.m.
PRICE RANGE: $

NEIGBORHHOOD: Sud-Ouest
Cute little shop selling ice cream, yogurt, and cookies. Customized ice cream sandwiches that display a creativity with the ingredients I'll bet you haven't seen before. Ginger molasses cookies with sunflower seed ice cream in the middle? That's what I mean.

DA GIOVANNI
572 Rue Sainte-Catherine Est, Montréal, 514-842-8851
CUISINE: Italian
DRINKS: Beer & Wine Only
SERVING: Lunch & Dinner
PRICE RANGE: $$
Here you'll find traditional Italian classics & pizza served in casual atmosphere.

DAMAS
1201 Av Van Horne, Montréal, 514-439-5435
www.restaurant-damas.com
CUISINE: Syrian
DRINKS: Full Bar
SERVING: Dinner
PRICE RANGE: $$
This beautiful Oriental-themed eatery offers a menu of authentic Middle Eastern cuisine. In fact, you won't find any better Middle Eastern cuisine anywhere in the U.S. My Menu Favorites include: Whole Mediterranean Sea Bass; Eggplant Stuffed with Lamb; and Pistachio and Walnut Lamb Kabab. The restaurant is filled with wonderful aromas that add to your dining experience. Take a second look at the wine list and you'll see entries from Turkey, Greece—all over the map. Ask them for a recommendation and try some of their unusual wines. You won't be able to fund them many places.

DE FARINE ET D'EAU FRAICHE
1701 Rue Amherst, Montréal, 514-703-6000
NO WEBSITE
CUISINE: Sandwiches / Bakery
DRINKS: No Booze
SERVING: Breakfast, Lunch, Open daily
PRICE RANGE: $$
Located in the gay village, here you'll find a friendly atmosphere and some of the best coffee in Montreal. My Menufeatures sandwiches, pastries, and light meals.

DINETTE TRIPLE CROWN
6704 Rue Clark, Montreal, 514-272-2617
www.dinettetriplecrown.com
CUISINE: Southern / American / Diner
DRINKS: Full Bar
SERVING: Lunch & Dinner daily, Closed Wed
PRICE RANGE: $$

This cute little eatery offers a menu of original Southern dishes that you won't find anywhere else in Montreal. Great takeout.

DOMINION SQUARE TAVERN
1243 Rue Metcalfe, Montreal, 514-564-5056
www.tavernedominion.com
CUISINE: Gastropub
DRINKS: Full Bar
SERVING: Dinner nightly, Lunch weekdays
PRICE RANGE: $$$
This beautiful gastropub with Victorian decorative flourishes offers Chef Eric Dupuis's European inspired menu. My Menu Favorites include: Braised Lamb Shank and Fish Terrine. The charcuterie here is house-made, and features items you won't fund on or the charcuterie platters, like pig's head terrine and duck ham. The atmosphere is warm and inviting but the food is the star.

EUROPEA
1065 Rue Montreal, Montreal, 514-398-9229
https://jeromeferrer.ca/
CUISINE: French / Polish
DRINKS: Full Bar
SERVING: Dinner
PRICE RANGE: $$$$
Languedoc-born Chef Jérôme Ferrer offers an inventive French menu in a beautiful 3-story townhouse setting which, despite the fact that he's built up somewhat of a culinary empire, remains his flagship location. There's a lovely 10-course tasting

menu for the adventurous and I heartily recommend it. Ferrer serves his food

with such a flourish, I always love coming here. (The foie gras comes out seared on a hot stone with a glass dome covering it. The waiter then dresses it with a caramelized sauce made of ice-wine, a Québeçois wine similar to Sauternes.) The first time you come here, you'll think the show might outshine the food, until of course you taste the food, and then all doubts vanish. Almost 1,000 selections on the ambitious wine list. Other Menu favorites include: Lobster cappuccino and the Blue cheese lollipops. Reservations recommended.

FANTASIE
1355 Rue Sainte-Catherine Est, Montreal, 514-523-3466
No Website
CUISINE: Japanese / Thai / Vietnamese
DRINKS: Full Bar
SERVING: Dinner
PRICE RANGE: $$$
This Vietnamese restaurant features a variety of Thai, Vietnamese and Cambodian influenced dishes.

FERREIRA CAFÉ
1446 Rue Peel, Montréal, 514-848-0988
www.ferreiracafe.com
CUISINE: Portuguese
DRINKS: Full Bar
SERVING: Dinner nightly
PRICE RANGE: $$$
This beautiful Mediterranean-themed eatery offers an impressive menu of fine Portuguese seafood. My

Menu Favorites include: Mushroom & Duck Risotto and Halibut Filet. Nice wine & port list.

FOXY
1638 Rue Notre-Dame Ouest, Montreal, 514-925-7007
www.foxy.restaurant/fr
CUISINE: Canadian (New)
DRINKS: Full bar
SERVING: Dinner nightly
PRICE RANGE: $$$$
NEIGHBORHOOD: Sud-Ouest
New restaurant from Olive and Gourmando, but offering a more rustic chic décor. Small menu (less than 15 items) with nightly specials. Favorites include: BBQ ribs and Cornish hen – most of the items cooked on the wood fired oven.

GARDE-MANGER
408 Rue Saint François Xavier, Montréal, 514-678-5044
www.crownsalts.com/gardemanger
CUISINE: Canadian cuisine
DRINKS: Full Bar
SERVING: Open Tues – Sun for dinner
PRICE RANGE: $$$$
This bar-like eatery run by the charismatic Chuck Hughes offers a menu with seafood-focused cuisine. But it's just as important to come here for the fun as it is for the food. The tattooed Hughes beat Bobby Flay on "Iron Chef" with a lobster *poutine*. This place is just off the Rue St. Paul on a side street. You'll always find a lively crowd here. My Menu Favorites include that very same Lobster *Poutine* mentioned above and Seared Scallops with roasted carrots.

Around the corner is another of Chuck's places, **Le Bremner**, also a great spot where the excitement is high but the food is serious.

GRINDER
1708 Rue Notre-Dame Ouest, Montréal, 514-439-1130
www.restaurantgrinder.ca/en
CUISINE: French / Steakhouse
DRINKS: Full Bar
SERVING: Lunch & Dinner daily, Closed Sun
PRICE RANGE: $$$
This beautifully designed little French eatery offers a comfortable atmosphere for dining. The menu features raw & cooked meats & seafood. They have unusual tartares: bison mixed with espresso butter and orange brunoise, for instance. My Menu Favorites include: Grilled Shrimp; Beef Short Ribs; a 40-ounce rib eye for 2. The wine list features an impressive list of boutique wines. Patio dining in the summer.

GRUMMAN '78
630 De Courcelle, Montreal, 514-290-5125
www.grumman78.com
CUISINE: Mexican
DRINKS: Full Bar
SERVING: Dinner, closed Tuesday
PRICE RANGE: $$
Trendy Mexican eatery located in a renovated garage off the beaten path in St.-Henri, offering a very creative menu specializing in tacos. Favorites include *banh mi* tacos, escargot quesadillas, salmon salad and Pulled pork tacos. Great cocktails.

HOF KELSTEN
4524 Blvd Saint Laurent, Montreal, 514-649-7991
www.hofkelsten.com
CUISINE: Bakery/Sandwiches
DRINKS: No Booze
SERVING: Breakfast, Lunch, Dinner; closed Mon & Tues
PRICE RANGE: $$

NEIGHBORHOOD: Plateau-Mont-Royal
Bakery and lovely café serving artisanal Jewish & French pastries, freshly baked breads and brunch. My favorite is the merguez sausage shakshuka. Or try the Challah French toast and the chocolate Babka.

HOOGAN ET BEAUFORT
4095 Rue Molson, Montreal, 514-903-1233
www.hooganetbeaufort.com
CUISINE: Canadian (New)/French
DRINKS: Full bar
SERVING: Lunch & Dinner; Dinner only on Sat; Closed Mondays
PRICE RANGE: $$
NEIGHBORHOOD: Rosemont-La Petite-Patrie
This relatively new eatery is located in an old factory where the Canadian Pacific Railway used to assemble its locomotives. One of the byproducts of hat original building is the fine looking high ceilings. Varied menu features entrees, pastas, and favorites like fire

grilled focaccia and Quebec mozzarella. Many items cooked on open fire pit. Nice choice for Sunday brunch (small plate menu).

HOTEL HERMAN
5171 Boulevard Saint-Laurent, Montréal, 514-278-7000
www.hotelherman.com
CUISINE: Gastropub / Tapas / Scandinavian
DRINKS: Full Bar
SERVING: Dinner nightly, Closed Tues
PRICE RANGE: $$
In Mile End you'll find the trendy Hotel Herman (not really a hotel) offers a creative seasonal menu of small plates from its hipster chefs. The gastropub features an intimate U-shaped bar that serves natural wines. The bartenders here concentrate on pre-Prohibition cocktails, which I love. My Menu Favorites include the popular Marinated trout with smoked crème fraîche and the roasted duck with rutabaga. (I wished more chefs served rutabaga, because I love it.) It's small and popular, so reservations are recommended.

JOE BEEF
2491 Rue Notre-Dame Quest, Montreal, 514-935-6504
www.joebeef.ca
CUISINE: Gastropub
DRINKS: Full Bar
SERVING: Dinner nightly, closed Mon
PRICE RANGE: $$$$
NEIGHBORHOOD: Little Burgundy

Located near the Historic Atwater market, this popular gastropub offers the Joe Beef Steak and my special favorite, the Lobster spaghetti. Their excellent wine selection is updated on a massive chalkboard that takes up a whole wall. Chefs David McMillan and Frédéric Morin have published a great cookbook, "The Art of Living According to Joe Beef." They have another eatery just a couple of doors down, **Liverpool House**, which is quite a bit cheaper than Joe Beef. Joe Beef, by the way, was the name of an Irish tavern owner back in the 1850s.

L'AUBERGE SAINT-GABRIEL
426 Rue Saint-Gabriel, Montreal, 514-878-3561
www.aubergesaint-gabriel.com
CUISINE: Canadian (New)
DRINKS: Full bar
SERVING: Dinner nightly, lunch Thursday & Friday, closed Sun & Mon
PRICE RANGE: $$$$
Owners Marc Bolay and Guy Laliberté (he was a founder of cirque du Soleil) have created a fine dining destination with a creative menu of Quebec cuisine. The location was built as a house for a French soldier in 1688, but later became an inn around 1753. It's considered to be the first inn in North America. It was given the first liquor license under British rule. The old stone walls and candle-lit fireplace create a warm atmosphere. Favorites include: Rabbit gazpacho, house made charcuterie boards, aged on site Beef tartare with truffle mayo. Nice wine list. Lounge and nightclub (in the basement) on premises.

L'AVENUE
922 Avenue du Mont Royal Est, Montréal, 514-523-8780
www.restaurantlavenue.ca/
CUISINE: Brunch / Burgers
DRINKS: Full Bar
SERVING: Breakfast/Brunch, Lunch, Dinner, Late Night
PRICE RANGE: $$
This is a great place for breakfast but be warned that the menu is only in French. The menu offers some creative selections including the vegetable omelet served with an arugula salad and Eggs Benedict made with smoked salmon.

L'ESCALIER
552 Rue Sainte-Catherine Est, Montreal, 514-419-6609
www.lescalier-montreal.com
CUISINE: Vegetarian / Music Venue
DRINKS: Full Bar
SERVING: Breakfast, Lunch, Late night
PRICE RANGE: $$

This is a mixture of a pub and a café. Comfortable atmosphere that actually feels like you're in someone's house. Great extensive vegetarian menu. Live music on certain nights. Cash only.

L'OEUFRIER
1702 Boulevard des Laurentides, Montreal, Laval, 450-667-4444
www.loeufrier.ca
CUISINE: Breakfast
DRINKS: No Booze
SERVING: Breakfast, Brunch
PRICE RANGE: $$
This popular breakfast place is always packed. Nice varied menu with generous portions. Waffles, pancakes, omelets, pastries, and great coffee.

LA MIE MATINALE BOULANGENRIE
1654 Rue Sainte-Catherine E, Montreal, 514-529-5656
www.lamiematinale.ca
CUISINE: Argentinean
DRINKS: No Booze
SERVING: Breakfast, Brunch, Lunch
PRICE RANGE: $$
This casual Argentinean eatery offers a pleasant outdoor area for people watching (weather permitting). Here you'll find a no-frills menu with sandwiches, homemade soups, salads, and pastries.

LA PIAZETTA
1101 Sainte-Catherine Rue E, Montreal, 514-526-2244
www.lapiazzetta.ca
CUISINE: Pizza

DRINKS: Full Bar
SERVING: Lunch, Dinner
PRICE RANGE: $$
This Quebec pizza chain made its name in the late '80s with their European-inspired thin-crust square pizza. Today they offer a variety of pizzas and have enlarged the menu to include salads, pastas, and gluten-free items. My Menu Favorites include: Creole pie and Seafood pizza. Desserts options include the Praline Royale, a light chocolate multi-layered mousse cake.

LABO CULINAIRE FOODLAB
1201 St. Laurent Blvd, Montreal, 514-844-2033
www.sat.qc.ca/fr/foodlab
CUISINE: Barbecue / Wine Bar / International
DRINKS: Full Bar
SERVING: Dinner; Tues - Fi
PRICE RANGE: $$$

Michelle Marek and Seth Gabrielse welcome guests to their unique Culinary Lab for an experience that won't be forgotten. It's situated on third floor of the swanky new media performance center of the Société des Arts Technologique. The menu changes every two weeks and comes from the two inventive chefs who are especially creative with baked goods. The menu at press time focused on dishes from Provence: mixed olives; Bouillabaisse Borgne; Assiette Aioli; Entrecote de Boeuf; Cerises Montmorency.

LALOUX
250 Avenue des Pins Est, Montreal, 514-287-9127
www.laloux.com
CUISINE: French
DRINKS: Full Bar
SERVING: Dinner nightly, Lunch weekdays
PRICE RANGE: $$$
This beautiful Parisian inspired white-tablecloth bistro serves French cuisine made with locally sourced products. Great wine pairings and gourmet desserts. My Menu Favorites include: Beef flank steak and Guinea fowl breast. Extensive wine list include a nice selection of French wines.

LARRY'S
9 Ave Fairmount E, Montreal, 514-708-1070
www.lawrencemtl.com
https://lawrencemtl.com/larrys/
CUISINE: American
DRINKS: Beer & Wine
SERVING: Breakfast, Lunch, Dinner 7 days
PRICE RANGE: $$

NEIGHBORHOOD: Plateau-Mont-Royal
Neighborhood eatery serving beautifully sourced and prepared dishes from only the best suppliers and at very reasonable prices in a casual atmosphere. When you come in here, you'll see the list of the farms and meat suppliers they use. They're up front about everything, from the lettuce to the pork. Really so much to choose from. My Favorites: King mushroom, lots of charcuterie dishes, lustrous salads, rare beef with chimichurri sauce. Located right around the corner from sister restaurant, the fancier, more elegant **Lawrence** (where I like the chorizo with smoked scallops), as well as **Boucherie Lawrence**, where they make the best sandwiches beginning at 11 till they run out of bread. Can't miss with any of these delightful spots.

LAVANDERIA
374 Avenue Victoria, Westmount, 514-303-4123
www.lavanderiaresto.com
CUISINE: Latin American
DRINKS: Full bar
SERVING: Dinner
PRICE RANGE: $$$$
NEIGHBORHOOD: Notre-Dame-de-Grâce
Chef Antonio Park offers a menu of Argentine cuisine featuring a variety of meats, pastas, and desserts in a restaurant he named after his dad's factory in

Argentina where he makes acid-washed jeans. Meat lovers like the Grill Assortment – a selection of sausage, lamb, chicken, sweetbreads, fish, and pork served on a grill, and it's no wonder because the chef uses a creative mixture of charcoal from Japan, Quebec and Argentina that throws off a unique flavor. He is also the only chef in Canada with a permit to import Kobe beef directly from the Hyogo Prefecture in Japan.

LAWRENCE
5201 Boulevard Saint-Laurent, Montréal, 514-503-1070
www.lawrencerestaurant.com
CUISINE: French
DRINKS: Full Bar
SERVING: Lunch & Dinner Wed-Sun; weekend Brunch; closed Mon & Tues
PRICE RANGE: $$$
British expat Marc Cohen offers a menu of refined French cuisine epitomizing the nose-to-tail school of cooking that results in such exotic menu items as rabbit offal tart and lamb's heart with prunes and bacon. The bar serves up inspired craft cocktails. My Menu Favorites include: Shellfish and Rouille on toast and Sandwich Oeuf and Saucisse. The French pastries are simply divine. Great French toast and

scones. This place is properly jammed at weekend Brunch, so be prepared for a wait.

LE BREMNER
361 Rue Saint-Paul Est, Montreal, 514-544-0446
www.crownsalts.com/lebremner
CUISINE: Seafood
DRINKS: Full Bar
SERVING: Dinner nightly, Closed Sun
PRICE RANGE: $$$
Be careful or you'll walk right by it (as I did). Down a few steps into a basement space is this hip eatery (run by Chuck Hughes of Garde Manger), quite intimate with only 30 seats in the dining room and 10 at the bar. The seafood menu is quite impressive. My Menu Favorites include: Fried Quail and Salmon Tartare. The wine menu is very impressive and a draw to wine lovers.

LE CHIEN FUMANT
4710 Rue de Lanaudière, Montréal, 514-524-2444
www.lechienfumant.com
CUISINE: Canadian cuisine / American / British cuisine
DRINKS: Full Bar
SERVING: Dinner daily, weekend brunch
PRICE RANGE: $$$
This eatery features an ever-changing unconventional menu that includes dishes like the Pulled Pork French Pain Perdu (French Toast) with Creamy Scrambled Eggs making it a favorite destination for Brunch. Everything is homemade here including the English muffins and real Southern-style biscuits.

LE FILET
219 Ave du Mont Royal Quest, Montreal, 514-360-6060
www.lefilet.ca
CUISINE: Seafood
DRINKS: Full Bar
SERVING: Dinner, Tues to Sat
PRICE RANGE: $$$
This fashionable hot spot at the base of Mont-Royal offers a creative seafood menu. Part of the restaurant group owned by Claude Pelltier, this place has quite a reputation to live up to and for the most part it makes the grade. The oysters here seem to have a brinier scent than elsewhere in town, and they are excellent when served with yuzu marmalade. Menu features Asian inspired seafood dishes. My Menu Favorites include: Crispy halibut and Linguini with clams,

grilled octopus; lamb medallions; Maritime oysters; house-cured gravlax; rock crab risotto. Bar list features primarily French wines. Seasonal terrace.

LE GOUT DE VIETNAM
1389 Rue Sainte-Catherine Est, Montréal, 514-523-9703
www.legoutduvietnam.com
CUISINE: Vietnamese
DRINKS: Full Bar
SERVING: Dinner
PRICE RANGE: $$
This casual eater offers a simple no-frills Vietnamese and Asian menu. My Menufavorite is the Lemongrass chicken. Lots of combos and daily specials.

LE MOUSSO
1023 Rue Ontario E, Montréal, 438-384-7410
https://lemousso.com
CUISINE: Canadian (New)
DRINKS: Full bar
SERVING: Dinner Wed – Sat; Closed Sun - Tues
PRICE RANGE: $$
NEIGHBORHOOD: Ville-Marie
This eatery offers a tasting menu featuring small plates of the chef's picks in a very edgy Brooklyn-style atmosphere, with seating either at tables or at a counter. Creative menu with dishes like Cotton candy with foie gras inside, Quebec Wagyu beef with caviar. Nice preparation of lamb – melts in your mouth. Interesting desserts like the Pomme sponge cake served with apple butter.

LE SERPENT
257, Rue Prince, Montréal, 514-316-4666
www.leserpent.ca
CUISINE: Canadian/Italian/French
DRINKS: Full bar
SERVING: Lunch & Dinner, closed Sun
PRICE RANGE: $$$
A beautiful restaurant with an industrial-chic feel. This is a must-stop for foodies with a creative menu offering a variety of cuisines. Favorites include: Lobster risotto and BBQ duck. Creative desserts like Lavender white chocolate with strawberry mousse.

LE VIN PAPILLON
2519 Rue Notre-Dame Ouest, Montréal, 514-439-6494
www.vinpapillon.com
CUISINE: Canadian cuisine / Wine Bar
DRINKS: Full Bar
SERVING: Dinner, Closed Sun & Mon
PRICE RANGE: $$

This cozy little wine bar offers a menu of creative, farm-fresh cuisine served Tapas style. The menu is heavy on the veggies. Celery root and bagna cauda (a sauce made with anchovies and garlic), chicken wings, and Mushrooms & potatoes from the grill, grilled white turnips, hummus made of hubbard squash & focaccia. Great desserts. Outdoor patio open during warmer months. The wines here emphasize quaffable Burgundies. No reservations, so come early.

LES 400 COUPS
400 Rue Notre-Dame Est, Montréal, 514-985-0400
www.les400coups.ca/en
CUISINE: French
DRINKS: Full Bar
SERVING: Dinner served daily
PRICE RANGE: $$$
This posh eatery offers Chef Guillaume Cantin's menu of refined French cuisine using local ingredients. It's a trifle costly and the portions are small, but they're extravagantly delicious. My Menu Favorites include: squash soup like you've never had squash soup before, delectable duck croquettes, Yellow Sturgeon and Guinea Fowl Breast. The pastry chef offers a divine selection of desserts, but my favorite is the lime curd, which mixes pistachios with gin, cucumbers, cilantro and vanilla. Yum.

LES TROIS BRASSEURS
732 Rue Sainte-Catherine Ouest, Montréal, 514-788-6333
www.les3brasseurs.ca
CUISINE: French / Gastropub
DRINKS: Full Bar
SERVING: Lunch, Dinner
PRICE RANGE: $$
The name, meaning three brewers, says it all. The beer is good and so is the food. The menu offers French fare based on recipes from the North. My

Menu Favorites include: Lamb Shank and Flatbread pizzas.

LEMÉAC
1045 Avenue Laurier O, Outremont, 514-270-0999
www.restaurantlemeac.com
CUISINE: French
DRINKS: Full Bar
SERVING: Lunch & Dinner
PRICE RANGE: $$$
French bistro popular among A-list crowd. I'm not certain if they come for the excellent food or the gorgeous waiters. Favorites include: Grilled Calamari, Zucchini and Tuna tartare, duck confit, raw oysters. It's a little cheaper if you come after 10 p.m. when a prix fixe menu goes into effect. Impressive selection of wines by the glass.

LIVERPOOL HOUSE
2501 Rue Notre-Dame Ouest, Montreal, 514-313-6049
www.joebeef.ca
CUISINE: French / Italian
DRINKS: Full Bar
SERVING: Dinner nightly, Closed Sun & Mon
PRICE RANGE: $$$$

Joe Beef's popular sister restaurant features a menu of market-inspired comfort dishes, an oyster bar, food from different cultures. It's just as busy and just as much fun as Joe Beef. My Menu Favorites include: the Liverpool Steak, an impressive 16 oz. piece of perfectly cooked meat; Lobster Spaghetti; Clams Casino; Ricotta Gnocchi; some British pub fare. The food is consistently good, no doubt because the kale, sorrel, basil and other leafy items come from a 2,000 square foot garden behind Joe Beef.

LOLA ROSA
4581 Rue Parc, Montreal, 514-843-5652
http://lolarosa.ca/en/park-ave-lola/
CUISINE: Vegetarian / Gluten-free
DRINKS: Full Bar

SERVING: Lunch & Dinner daily
PRICE RANGE: $$
This great little restaurant has a creative décor and is filled with artwork. My Menu Favorites include: Quesadilla and the Vegi-burger. Great dessert choices like the very rich banana chocolate cake.

MACHE
1655 Rue Saint-Denis, Montréal, 514-439-5535
www.restaurantmache.com
CUISINE: American / Canadian cuisine
DRINKS: Beer & Wine
SERVING: Lunch & Dinner, Open daily
PRICE RANGE: $$
This casual eatery offers a menu of Canadian and American comfort food. My Menu Favorites include: Shepherd's Pie and Poutines. The portions are large here so bring your appetite.

MAESTRO SVP
3615 Boulevard Saint-Laurent, Montréal, 514-842-6447
www.maestrosvp.com
CUISINE: Seafood / Tapas
DRINKS: Full Bar
SERVING: Dinner nightly
PRICE RANGE: $$$
Located in a trendy area of Montreal, this eatery offers a welcoming atmosphere and an impressive menu. My Menu Favorites include: Crab cakes and Baked Oysters St Jacques. Nice choice for a date night.

MAISON BOULUD
1228 Sherbrooke Ouest, Montreal, 514-842-4224
www.maisonboulud.com
CUISINE: French (with a few Italian twists)
DRINKS: Full bar
SERVING: Lunch & Dinner; Sunday breakfast
PRICE RANGE: $$$$
NEIGHBORHOOD: Ville-Marie
Located at the historic Ritz Carlton (should I say more?) but since it's named after renowned chef Daniel Boulud it must be good. Every dish is a work of art and every meal is an experience – elegant French cuisine at its best. The charming location in this excellent hotel overlooks a garden and a duck pond—try your damnedest to get a table with this view. Favorites include: Homemade potato Gnocchi with Lobster and Snow crab served with razor clam salad; ravioli filled with sheep's milk; housemade

paté; guinea fowl leg confit. Reservations recommended.

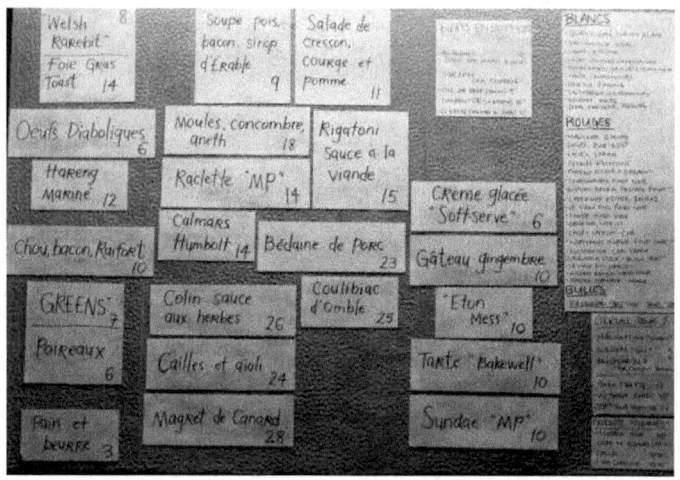

MAISON PUBLIQUE
4720 Rue Marquette, Montréal, 514-507-0555
www.maisonpublique.com
CUISINE: Gastropub / Brunch
DRINKS: Full Bar
SERVING: Dinner nightly, Lunch Sat & Sun, Closed Mon & Tues
PRICE RANGE: $$

Derek Dammann offers a menu of market-fresh pub dishes in a bar atmosphere. The kitchen is open so you can see the chef cooking if you sit at the bar. The menu changes seasonally as the food is prepared from fresh produce bought locally. Try the Fennel Sausages; Baked Oysters; the Welsh Rarebit; Duck Steak (for 2); Sockeye Salmon. Not only is the food local, but the wines are, too, featuring Canadian wines. (Yes, Blanche, they make wines in Canada, and very good ones, too.) Nice choice for weekend Brunch.

MANANA
3605 rue Saint-Denis, Montreal, 514-847-1050
No web site
CUISINE: Mexican
DRINKS: Full Bar
SERVING: Lunch, Dinner, Open daily
PRICE RANGE: $$
If you want authentic Mexican cuisine, this is definitely the place. Here you'll find an extensive menu featuring items like the Bean Burrito that comes with fried eggplant, rice, and guacamole. The margaritas are the best.

MANITOBA
271 rue Saint Zotique Ouest, 514-270-8000
www.restaurantmanitoba.com
CUISINE: Canadian (New)
DRINKS: Full bar
SERVING: Dinner nightly
PRICE RANGE: $$$$
NEIGHBORHOOD: Rosemont-La Petite-Patrie
Contemporary eatery located in an industrial setting punctuated with animal furs and logs to give it a rustic look, Manitoba has chalkboards listing a creative menu of New Canadian cuisine with a focus on locally sourced ingredients. Menu choices include: Venison and Mackerel. Desserts choices are just as interesting like the Prune Custard pie. Many of their signature cocktails are created with their own honey they make (well, that their bees make) on the roof of this building.

MOISHES
3961 Boulevard Saint-Laurent, Montréal, 514-845-3509
www.moishes.ca
CUISINE: Steakhouse; Jewish cuisine
DRINKS: Full Bar
SERVING: Dinner nightly
PRICE RANGE: $$$$

This popular steakhouse (it's been around for decades, and never gets stale, only better) offers a menu of charbroiled meats and Jewish sides. The dark wood paneling and sparkling chandeliers throw off a formal mood that makes you feel important the minute you stroll in. Get the chopped liver starter—it's the best you've had in quite a while, I'll guarantee it. Other great choices are the bone-in filet mignon, a cut you rarely see. If you want something more substantial get the char-grilled rib eye. The Jewish sides are excellent as well: boiled or fried verenikas (pockets of dough filled with ham, cheese, just about anything), potato latkes, Karnatzlach (a sausage that's really more like Middle Eastern kefta kebabs than sausage) and sweetbreads.

MON LAPIN
150 Rue Saint-Zotique E, Montreal, No phone
CUISINE: Wine Bar
DRINKS: Wine only
SERVING: Dinner
PRICE RANGE: $$
NEIGHBORHOOD: Rosemont-La Petite-Patrie

Small chic wine bar that opens nightly at 5 p.m. in the area north of trendy Mile End. No reservations accepted so there's usually a line. (They only have bout 30 seats.) Five seats are at the bar overlooking the open kitchen. Small room, but still comfortable and cozy, the walls covered with paintings of rustic scenes with forests, rabbits, hunting scenes. Menu includes unusual organic wines and ciders, and a menu of small plates based heavily on seasonal ingredients. Menu picks: Scallops with rhubarb sauce and Smoked eel carbonera pasta. Menu changes daily.

MONTREAL POOL ROOM
1217 Saint-Laurent Blvd, Montreal, 514-954-4487
No Web Site
CUISINE: Comfort Food/Hot Dogs
DRINKS: Full bar
SERVING: Lunch

PRICE RANGE: $
NEIGHBORHOOD: Ville-Marie
Dating back to 1912, it's no wonder this is a well-known and frequently busy greasy spoon located in Montreal's former red-light district. Famous for their Hot Dogs (served steamed or grilled). Popular among the artsy crowd. Don't get fooled by the name – there are no pool tables here, though there used to be a long time ago. It's sign is not as interesting as the one across the street at Café Cleopatre, which indicates you can enjoy "stripteaseuses" as well as "danseuses a gogo."

MOZZA
1326 Rue Sainte-Catherine Est, Montréal, 514-524-0295
www.restaurantmozza.ca
CUISINE: Canadian cuisine / Italian
DRINKS: Beer & Wine

SERVING: Dinner nightly
PRICE RANGE: $$
This popular eatery offers a simple Italian menu (mostly pizza & pasta) that happens to be written in French. Waitresses are available for translations and suggestions. Menu favorites include: Escargot in a pink sauce and Cream pasta with Jumbo shrimps.

NORA GRAY
1391 Rue Saint-Jacques, 514-419-6672
www.noragray.com
CUISINE: Italian
DRINKS: Full Bar
SERVING: Dinner, Closed Sun & Mon
PRICE RANGE: $$$$
Very upscale eatery in Griffintown with a menu of classic Southern Italian & Sicilian dishes. Menu favorites include: Halibut w/fresh corn polenta; Braised rabbit ravioli; Lemon sausage with crushed potatoes and zucchini chips. You can't leave without trying their dessert special, a homemade doughnut with peach marmalade and mascarpone. The bar serves inspired cocktails and offers an impressive wine list.

NUDO
1055 Boulevard Saint-Laurent, Montréal, 514-508-9636
http://nudomontreal.com/
CUISINE: Chinese
DRINKS: No Booze
SERVING: Lunch & Dinner daily
PRICE RANGE: $

This restaurant offers a new interpretation of Chinese cuisine. Menu favorites include: Beef tripe and Braised Beef shank.

OLIVE ET GOURMANDO
351 Rue Saint Paul Ouest, Montréal, 514-350-1083
www.oliveetgourmando.com
CUISINE: Bakery / Sandwiches
DRINKS: No Booze
SERVING: Breakfast, Lunch & Dinner, Closed Sun & Mon
PRICE RANGE: $$
This spot is popular among foodies who love to dine on artisanal breads & sweets. People staying in the boutique hotels in nearby Ols Montreal swarm here. Menu features a nice variety of salads and Paninis (the egg Panini is tasty), crab cakes. This place has the best baked goods in the neighborhood: scones with cherries and ginger; banana & walnut muffins. Perfect place to gather items for a picnic.

OTHYM
1112 Blvd De Maisonneuve E, Montreal, 514-525-3443
www.othym.com
CUISINE: French
DRINKS: BYOB
SERVING: Lunch, Dinner
PRICE RANGE: $$$
This friendly eatery offers a great selection of French cuisine. Menu favorites include Filet Mignon and Riz de Veau. The décor is beautiful with red brick and white walls and 14-foot ceilings. Daily specials.

PASTAGA
6389 Boulevard Saint-Laurent, Montréal, 438-381-6389
www.pastaga.ca
CUISINE: Brasserie / French / Tapas
DRINKS: Full Bar
SERVING: Dinner nightly, Lunch Fri & Sun
PRICE RANGE: $$$
Chef Martin Juneau offers a creative menu of Montreal-inspired small plates. The wine list is filled with natural wines that will impress. Menu favorites include: Pork & Pancake; Arctic Char; White Tuna. Delicious dessert selection.

PATRICE PATISSIER
2360 Rue Notre-Dame St W, Local 104, Montreal, 514-439-5434
www.patricepatissier.ca
CUISINE: Bakery/Cafe
DRINKS: No Booze

SERVING: Lunch & Dinner; closed Mon & Tues
PRICE RANGE: $$
NEIGBORHHOOD: Sud-Ouest

In Little Burgundy you'll find this modern bakery and coffee shop serving decadent pastries. (What other kind would you want?) Their Choux a la Crème is perfection (a mixture of caramel, chocolate and banana cream pastry). There's an excellent brunch here—my favorite dish is the baked eggs with sausage they make on premise, but there's plenty more.

POUDING CAFÉ
1227a Rue Amherst Montreal, 514-510-7991
No Website
CUISINE: French
DRINKS: Full Bar

SERVING: Breakfast/ Lunch, Open daily except Sat
PRICE RANGE: $$
This popular neighborhood café offers a simple menu of primarily comfort food and sandwiches but there are a few gluten-free options.

PROVISIONS 1268
1268 Avenue Van Horne, Montreal, 514-508-0828
www.restaurantprovisions.ca
CUISINE: Canadian cuisine
DRINKS: Full Bar
SERVING: Dinner nightly, Closed Sun & Mon
PRICE RANGE: $$$
This elegant but intimate eatery (only 30 seats) offers a creative menu made with local ingredients. It's got modern art on the walls (a Picasso, screens from the Iranian Pavilion at Expo 67). The place is so small the chef prepares each plate himself. The menu is very brief, but very good. Popular dishes include: Beef tartare with oyster espuma and Duck Magret. Great

selection of desserts like the white chocolate, sour cherry ice cream. Take a trip to the bathroom even if you don't have to just so you can see the Japanese toilet: it uses a blow-dryer.

PULLMAN
3424, Avenue du Parc, Montreal, 514-288-7779
www.pullman-mtl.com
CUISINE: Tapas
DRINKS: Full bar
SERVING: Dinner
PRICE RANGE: $$
Great wine bar with an impressive offering (over 300 bottles and 50 wines by the glass). Ask one of their friendly sommeliers for a "trio," which is a 2-ounce pour of 3 wines. Great way to sample their selection. They also have a very tasty a tapas menu. Favorites include: Bison sliders, grilled cheddar sandwiches, sea bass carpaccio, foie gras, smoked meat terrine and Lemon squares for dessert.

QING HUA
1019 Boulevard Saint-Laurent, Montréal, 514-903-9887
No Website
CUISINE: Chinese
DRINKS: Beer only
SERVING: Lunch & Dinner daily
PRICE RANGE: $$ / CASH ONLY
This is a casual Chinese eatery that attracts the university crowd. Simple menu with a variety of choices. The huge variety of dumplings is a great draw here, with unusual offerings like chopped pork

and sea urchin. Too weird? Go for the shrimp and squash dumplings. Everything here's delicious. Once I got started, I was popping those dumplings like candy. Cash only.

QUARTIER GENERAL
1251 Rue Gilford, Montréal, 514-658-1839
www.lequartiergeneral.ca
CUISINE: French
DRINKS: BYOB
SERVING: Dinner nightly, Lunch weekdays
PRICE RANGE: $$$
This busy upscale bistro offers up an impressive menu of French cuisine. Menu favorites include: Cote de Veau de la Plaine (Veal Shank) with Foie Gras and Seared Foie Gras. Note: this is a bring your own wine eatery.

RÉSONANCE CAFÉ
5175 Av du Parc, Montréal, 514-360-9629

www.resonancecafe.com
CUISINE: Vegetarian/Vegan
DRINKS: Full Bar
SERVING: Lunch & Dinner
PRICE RANGE: $$

Popular lounge with live entertainment – mostly jazz and blues – with a creative menu of mostly vegan dishes attracting a young a hip crowd. A lot of them are musicians on a budget. Come here and feel cool. Favorites include: BLT (tempeh bacon) and the Channa bowl. Nice selection of beverages including loose leaf teas and smoothies.

RESERVOIR
9 Avenue Duluth Est, Montréal, 514-849-7779
www.brasseriereservoir.ca
CUISINE: Pubs / Tapas / Small Plates
DRINKS: Full Bar
SERVING: Dinner/Late nights; open daily

PRICE RANGE: $$
This neighborhood pub offers a simple bar menu featuring a variety of sandwiches and snacks. Great place for weekend brunch.

RESTAURANT ALEP
199 Rue Jean-Talon Est, Montréal, 514-270-6396
www.restaurantalep.com
CUISINE: Syrian - Armenian
DRINKS: Full Bar
SERVING: Dinner
PRICE RANGE: $$$
They've been dishing up Syrian-Armenian cuisine to locals for decades here at Alep. Here the menu features Middle Eastern treats like the intricately spiced Syrian-Armenian mezze (appetizers) and kabobs. My advice when trying food you're unfamiliar with is to get a bunch of appetizers so you'll appreciate the variety. They will be happy to suggest things to you. (I like the moutabal, which is a mixture of eggplant and tahini.) Great smells emanate from the kitchen here. Impressive wine list.

RESTAUANT BASHA
930 Rue Sainte-Catherine O, Montreal, 514-866-4272
www.basharestaurant.com
CUISINE: Middle Eastern / Greek
DRINKS: No Booze
SERVING: Lunch, Dinner, Open daily
PRICE RANGE: $
This cafeteria-style eatery offers a great selection of meats, salads, vegetarian dishes, hummus and falafels.

RESTAURANT BONAPARTE
443 Rue Saint François Xavier, Montréal, 514-844-4368
www.restaurantbonaparte.com/en/
CUISINE: French
DRINKS: Full Bar
SERVING: Lunch weekdays, Dinner nightly
PRICE RANGE: $$$$
Located in an elegant Napoleon-themed inn, this French eatery offers gourmet tasting and pre-theatre menus. Menu favorites include: Lobster salad and Brushetta.
Don't leave without tasting the delicious chocolate mousse.

RESTAURANT CARTE BLANCHE
1159 Ontario Rue E, Montreal, 514-313-8019
www.restaurant-carteblanche.com
CUISINE: French
DRINKS: Full Bar

SERVING: Lunch & Dinner, Closed Sun & Mon
PRICE RANGE: $$$
André Loiseau's beautifully designed eatery offers two prix-fixe menus featuring refined seasonal French cuisine. Small wine list.

RESTAURANT THAILANDAIS BATO THAI
1694 Rue Sainte-Catherine E, Montreal, 514-524-6705
No Website
CUISINE: Thai
DRINKS: No Booze
SERVING: Lunch, Dinner
PRICE RANGE: $$
Popular Thai eatery with a menu of delicious food like the red curry shrimp late and pad Thai. Menu favorites include: Chicken peanut butter, Red Curry and Lemon Grass Soup.

ROBIN DES BOIS
4653 St Laurent, Montréal, 514-288-1010
www.robindesbois.ca
CUISINE: French
DRINKS: Full Bar
SERVING: Lunch & Dinner, Closed Sun
PRICE RANGE: $$
With the proceeds going to local charities, this place is staffed mainly by volunteers. Nice French menu. Menu favorites include: Braised Pork roast with Spatzl and Gnocchi with butternut squash. Great dessert selection.

SAINT HENRI MICRO TORREFACTEUR
3632 Rue Notre-Dame O, Montreal, 514-507-9696
www.sainthenri.ca
CUISINE: Coffee
DRINKS: No Booze
SERVING: 7:30 – 8 p.m. weekdays, 8:30 – 8 p.m. weekends
PRICE RANGE: $
NEIGBORHHOOD: Sud-Ouest
Popular café featuring house-roasted craft espresso and a nice selection of pastries. Impressive selection of herbal teas.

ST. VIATEUR BAGEL
263 Rue St-Viateur Ouest, Montreal, 514-276-8044
www.stviateurbagel.com
CUISINE: Bagels
DRINKS: No Booze
SERVING: 24 hours
PRICE RANGE: $
Popular Montreal-style bagel bakery serving fresh bagels made on the premises.

SALOON
1333 Rue Sainte-Catherine Est, Montréal, 514-522-1333
www.lesaloon.ca
CUISINE: Supper club / Global Fusion
DRINKS: Full Bar
SERVING: Lunch & Dinner
PRICE RANGE: $$
This is a combination supper club and bar. Varied menu includes grilled meats, pastas, pizzas, and salads. Their impressive brunch menu includes a page of exotic juices and smoothies. Menu favorites include: Parisian Eggs Benedict (they have a whole page dedicated to Eggs Benedict).

TABLA VILLAGE
1329 Rue Sainte-Catherine Est, Montréal, 514-523-6464
www.tablarestaurant.com

CUISINE: Indian
DRINKS: Full Bar
SERVING: Lunch & Dinner, Open daily
PRICE RANGE: $$
Attractive Indian eatery offers a menu of specials and Indian beer. The food is highly rated and not too spicy unless requested. Patio seating in the summer.

TAVERNE F
1485 rue Jeanne-Mance, Montréal, 514-289-4558
www.tavernef.com
CUISINE: Mediterranean
DRINKS: Full Bar
SERVING: Lunch weekdays, Dinner nightly
PRICE RANGE: $$$
This Portuguese Brasserie features a small plate menu in an intimate dining atmosphere. Menu favorites include: Pork Confit and Taverne Poutine. Nice selection of desserts for those with a sweet tooth.

TIM HORTON'S
159 Saint-Antoine Rue W, Montreal, 514-871-1509
www.timhortons.com
CUISINE: Deli/Sandwiches
DRINKS: Full Bar
SERVING: Breakfast, Lunch, & Dinner
PRICE RANGE: $
This popular Canadian diner is known for its coffee and doughnuts. Good breakfast spot and great selection of sandwiches (eat in or to go).

TITANIC
445 Rue Saint Pierre, Montréal, 514-849-0894
www.titanicmontreal.com
CUISINE: Café
DRINKS: No Booze
SERVING: Breakfast & Lunch, Closed Sat & Sun
PRICE RANGE: $$
This casual café offers a simple menu of creative sandwiches, salads, soups and homemade desserts.

TORTERIA LUPITA
4601 Rue Notre-Dame O, Montreal, 514-989-8464
www.torterialupita.com
CUISINE: Mexican/Sandwiches
DRINKS: Full Bar
SERVING: Lunch/Dinner; closed Sun & Mon
PRICE RANGE: $
NEIGBORHHOOD: Sud-Ouest/St-Henri

Cute little Mexican family opened and operated eatery ideal for and cheap and delicious lunch. Simple menu. My Favorites: Chicken flauta and Vegetarian smoked mozzarella. Try the deep fired churros for dessert. Takeout counter.

TOQUÉ!
900 Place Jean-Paul-Riopelle, Montréal, 514-499-2084
www.restaurant-toque.com
CUISINE: French
DRINKS: Full Bar
SERVING: Lunch & Dinner daily, Closed Sun & Mon
PRICE RANGE: $$$$
Renowned chef Normand Laprise offers his menu of delicious farm-fresh French cuisine. He was instrumental in the 1990s when he led the wave toward using local ingredients in his cooking, working with ground cherries, sea buckthorn, eels from Kamouraska, which is where he is from, on the south side of the St. Lawrence River. Menu favorites include: Leg of Lamb and Quail & Sausage, but the best option here is to go for the 7-course tasting menu. Get the wine parings as well. This is one of the best wine lists in all of Montreal.

WILENSKY'S LIGHT LUNCH
34 Avenue Fairmount Ouest, Montréal, +1 514-271-0247
www.wilenskys.com
CUISINE: Deli / Jewish
DRINKS: No Booze

SERVING: Breakfast & Lunch daily, Closed Sun
PRICE RANGE: $$

This family-owned Jewish deli has been serving the community delicious grilled sandwiches and snacks since 1932. You'll be lucky to snag one of the 9 wooden stools at the counter. The best thing to do here is order the "Special," which will get you piles of salami and bologna on a grilled *pletzel* roll (like a Kaiser roll) that's been generously swathed with mustard—it's served on a napkin. You pay when you're served, and you don't leave a tip because founder Moe Bolshevik never permitted it. Try the sodas made with syrup at the bar right before your eyes. There's a Brooklyn deli called the Mile High that serves a "Ruth Wilensky Special," but it costs twice as much as the one served here where it was created. So take that, Brooklyn!

Food Markets

MAISONNEUVE MARKET
4445 Ontario St. East (corner of William and David Ontario), 514-937-7754
www.marchespublics-mtl.com
Located in the borough of Mercier-Hochelaga-Maisonneuve, this market opened in the early 20th century in a majestic stone building. A large number of farmers, grocers, butchers and fishmongers followed each other for half a century. Closed in the

1960s by the municipality. But neighborhood residents saw to it that the Maisonneuve market gardening activity resumed in 1980. There was a wait of fifteen years the full market to be reborn in a new building, just a short walk from the old building. Open all year.

DID YOU FIND AN INTERESTING PLACE?
If you discover a place you think I should check out on my next visit, drop me a line, will you? I'll mention your name if I end up listing it.
andrewdelaplaine@mac.com

Atwater Market exterior

MARCHÉ ATWATER
138 Ave Atwater (at Notre Dame), 514-937-2863
www.marchespublics-mtl.com
Located in the southwest of Montreal, near the Lachine Canal, Atwater Market takes its name from the street that borders it and that memorializes Edwin Atwater, a businessman and alderman of the 19th century. The market has existed since 1933 and its architecture, art deco, it ranked among the most beautiful buildings in Montreal. Open all year, the market is famous for its many butchers and cheesemongers, horticultural producers in the spring, but also for its market gardens, which are installed on the perimeter of the building in the
summer. Shopkeepers offer a nice variety of fresh, refined and original products. There is also a center of

flavors, access to fast food, innovative and tastiest. The expertise comes merchants generations that have followed behind the stalls and succession working hard to perpetuate the reputation of the Atwater Market.

Atwater Market stall (below)

MARCHÉ JEAN-TALON
7070 Ave Henri Julien
www.marchespublics-mtl.com
Located in the heart of Little Italy, the Jean-Talon Market is one of the oldest public markets in Montreal. Opened in May 1933, it was first called the "North Market" before becoming, in 1983, the Jean-Talon Market, in honor of the first Intendant of New France.
The Jean-Talon market is characterized by a large collection of local producers of fruits and vegetables, as well as a wide range of shopkeepers. This is one of the largest North American markets, and is open year round.

Stall at Jean-Talon

LACHINE
1875 rue Notre-Dame
www.marchespublics-mtl.com
Located close to the bike path of the Lachine Canal, the Lachine Market has a long and rich history. It is the oldest public market in Montreal. Opened in 1845 on the site of the present borough hall, it is the heart of the economic center of the city. Destroyed by fire in 1866, the market reopened forty years later on Notre Dame.

INDEX

A

ACCORDS, 11
AGRIKOL, 12
ALEP, 68
American, 25, 45, 52
AMIR, 13
Argentinean, 14, 38
Armenian, 68
ARTHUR'S NOSH BAR, 14
AU PIED DE COCHON, 14

B

Bagels, 71
Bakery, 25, 61, 62
Barbecue, 39
BASHA, 68
BEAUTY'S, 14
BIG IN JAPAN, 15
BORIS BISTRO, 16
Boucherie Lawrence, 41
BOUILLON BILK, 17
Brasserie, 19, 62
BRASSERIE BERNARD, 18
BRASSERIE T, 19
Breakfast, 14, 37, 61
British cuisine, 45
Brunch, 36, 43, 54
Burgers, 36
BUVETTE CHEZ DIMONE, 20
BYBLOS LE PETIT CAFÉ, 21

C

Cafe, 62
Café, 20, 21, 74
CAFÉ LES ENTRETIENS, 21
CAFÉ SANTROPOL, 22
Canadian, 47
Canadian (New), 14, 18, 29, 33, 35, 46, 56
Canadian cuisine, 17, 21, 30, 45, 48, 52, 59, 64
CARTE BLANCHE, 69
Chinese, 60, 65
CHIPOLE & JALAPENO, 22
Coffee, 71
Comfort Food, 58
CREMERIE DALLA ROSE, 22

D

DA GIOVANNI, 23
DAMAS, 24
DE FARINE ET D'EAU FRAICHE, 25
Deli, 75
Deli/Sandwiches, 73
Diner, 14, 25
DINETTE TRIPLE CROWN, 25
DOMINION SQUARE TAVERN, 26

E

EUROPEA, 26

F

Fairmont Bagel, 7
FANTASIE, 28
FERREIRA CAFÉ, 28
FOXY, 29
French, 11, 16, 18, 19, 26, 31, 33, 40, 43, 47, 49, 50, 51, 53, 62, 63, 66, 69, 70, 75
Frozen Yogurt, 22

G

GARDE-MANGER, 30
Gastropub, 26, 34, 49, 54
Global Fusion, 72
Gluten-free, 51
Greek, 68
GRINDER, 31
GRUMMAN '78, 32

H

Haitian, 12
HOF KELSTEN, 32
HOOGAN ET BEAUFORT, 33
Hot Dogs, 58
HOTEL HERMAN, 34

I

Ice cream, 22
Indian, 73
Italian, 23, 47, 51, 59, 60

J

Japanese, 15, 28
Jewish cuisine, 57
JOE BEEF, 34

L

L'AUBERGE SAINT-GABRIEL, 35

L'AVENUE, 36
L'ESCALIER, 36
L'OEUFRIER, 37
La Banquise, 6
LA MIE MATINALE BOULANGENRIE, 38
LA PIAZETTA, 38
LABO CULINAIRE FOODLAB, 39
LACHINE, 82
LALOUX, 40
LARRY'S, 40
Latin American, 41
LAVANDERIA, 41
Lawrence, 41
LAWRENCE, 43
LE BREMNER, 44
LE CHIEN FUMANT, 45
LE FILET, 45
LE GOUT DE VIETNAM, 46
LE MOUSSO, 46
LE SERPENT, 47
LE VIN PAPILLON, 48
Lebanese, 13
LEMEAC, 50
LES 400 COUPS, 49
LES TROIS BRASSEURS, 49
LIVERPOOL HOUSE, 51
LOLA ROSA, 51

M

MA NANA, 55
MACHE, 52
MAESTRO SVP, 52
Main Deli Steakhouse, 7
MAISON BOULUD, 53
MAISON PUBLIQUE, 54
MAISONNEUVE MARKET, 77
MANITOBA, 56
MARCHÉ ATWATER, 79
MARCHÉ JEAN-TALON, 81

Mediterranean, 73
Mexican, 22, 32, 55, 74
Middle Eastern, 21, 68
MOISHES, 57
MON LAPIN, 57
MONTREAL POOL ROOM, 58
MOZZA, 59

N

NORA GRAY, 60
NUDO, 60

O

OLIVE ET GOURMANDO, 61
OTHYM, 62

P

PASTAGA, 62
Patati Patata, 6
PATRICE PATISSIER, 62
Pizza, 38
Polish, 26
Portugalia, 8
Portuguese, 28
POUDING CAFÉ, 63
PROVISIONS 1238, 64
Pubs, 67
PULLMAN, 65

Q

QING HUA, 65
QUARTIER GENERAL, 66

R

RESERVOIR, 67
RESONANCE CAFÉ, 66
RESTAURANT BONAPARTE, 69
ROBIN DES BOIS, 70
Rotisserie Romados, 8

S

SAINT HENRI MICRO TORREFACTEUR, 71
SALOON, 72
Sandwiches, 25, 61, 74
Scandinavian, 34
Schwartz's Montreal Hebrew Delicatessen, 7
Seafood, 44, 45, 52
Small Plates, 67
Southern, 25
ST. VIATEUR BAGEL, 71
Steakhouse, 31, 57
St-Viateur Bagel, 7
Supper club, 72
Syrian, 24, 68

T

TABLA VILLAGE, 72
Tapas, 20, 34, 48, 52, 62, 65, 67
TAVERN F, 73
Thai, 28, 70
THAILANDAIS BATO THAI, 70
TIM HORTON'S, 73
TITANIC, 74
TOQUE!, 75
TORTERIA LUPITA, 74

V

Vegan, 67
Vegetarian, 22, 36, 51, 67
Vietnamese, 28, 46

W

WILENSKY'S LIGHT LUNCH, 75
Wine Bar, 11, 20, 39, 48

WANT 3 **FREE** THRILLERS?

Why, of course you do!
If you like these writers--
Vince Flynn, Brad Thor, Tom Clancy, James Patterson, David Baldacci, John Grisham, Brad Meltzer, Daniel Silva, Don DeLillo
If you like these TV series –
House of Cards, Scandal, West Wing, The Good Wife, Madam Secretary, Designated Survivor

> You'll love the **unputdownable** series about
> Jack Houston St. Clair, with political intrigue, romance, and loads of action and suspense.

Besides writing travel books, I've written political thrillers for many years that have delighted hundreds of thousands of readers. I want to introduce you to my work!
Send me an email and I'll send you a link where you can download the first 3 books in my bestselling series, absolutely FREE.

Mention **this book** when you email me.
andrewdelaplaine@mac.com

www.ingramcontent.com/pod-product-compliance
Lightning Source LLC
LaVergne TN
LVHW051509070426
835507LV00022B/3020